Letter from a Woman with Borderline Personality Disorder

K. Marie

Published by Caos Hermoso, 2023.

While every precaution has been taken in the preparation of this book, the publisher assumes no responsibility for errors or omissions, or for damages resulting from the use of the information contained herein.

LETTER FROM A WOMAN WITH BORDERLINE PERSONALITY DISORDER

First edition. September 1, 2023.

ISBN: 979-8223774617

Written by K. Marie.

Table of Contents

*To all those who suffer from an extreme need of receiving
and giving love and to those who care enough to love us*

This is for you

Introduction

If you are reading this book, then you believe that the person you love is worth the effort required to understand the complex situation they find themselves in. It is a complex situation and not an easy journey. People with Borderline Personality Disorder struggle with relationships, but they also value relationships immensely, and this makes it possible to enjoy a good relationship.

If you love someone with Borderline Personality Disorder, then we want to help you learn to love them in a way that will protect and nurture your relationship.

Every relationship involves unique individuals. Some say that those with Borderline Personality Disorder are a little too unique. But there is no such thing as more unique, or less unique. People with this disorder are just generally more emotional. These heightened emotional states make everything look different. But with some education and a peek into their inner world, you could make appropriate decisions, and work towards a happier relationship. It is possible, and there is hope.

People with Borderline Personality Disorder can be difficult to be close to. They can be too hot, or too cold, too close, or too far. Seemingly little things can trigger someone into lashing out at you, and you could be at a loss as to how to deal with this. Is your relationship too intense, unpredictable, or just too complex? Are you trying to understand your partner, friend, or family member, but finding it difficult to get the answers you need?

If you've built a strong relationship, but are experiencing angry outbursts, you may be wondering how to handle this. You may value someone who has Borderline Personality Disorder, but you may dislike the disorder.

If you're in a family relationship with someone, you may be worried about their safety. You may feel like you're in the dark about what they're going through with the disorder, as they may not have the courage to share their inner world with you.

This book includes vulnerable real-life experiences of those with Borderline Personality Disorder. It talks to partners, family, and friends. It unpacks the way some of the symptoms or traits play out in reality, what they feel like, what makes it better, and what makes it worse. It lets you into the heart of people with the disorder, but it does so in a safe space where you can explore at your own pace.

The purpose of letting you into this inner world is to give you more context for your relationship issues. It will allow you to see from the perspective of those who walk the journey. It includes thoughts and feelings that are normally difficult for people to share, because of the vulnerability in close relationships, as well as because of the trust issues that are part of the baggage of Borderline Personality Disorder. Another reason people don't talk about it is because of the stigma unrightfully attached to it. The stigma is destructive and blocks awareness. But it is possible for people to share their secret feelings, insights, and hopes in the pages of a book. They can write like no one is watching them because no one is watching them!

The book uses easy language to navigate a difficult subject. It offers you perspective, clarity, and support. With knowledge and empathy, it is possible to enjoy good relationships with those you love who may be living with the disorder. The book will help to:

- Understand Borderline Personality Disorder from a personal perspective

- Know what you can do and what to avoid to improve your relationship with your loved one

- Know how to take care of yourself in your relationship with a person with Borderline Personality Disorder.

Every relationship you are in involves you and should consider you. It is important to include conscious self-care in your relationships with your loved ones. It is particularly important to take care of yourself in intense relationships which can be very rewarding, but also have the potential to be draining. Thank you for joining us on the vulnerable journey of creating stronger relationships.

Chapter 1: What is Borderline Personality Disorder?

What are the symptoms?

The following are the 9 symptoms of Borderline Personality Disorder, according to the DSM 5 (the fifth edition of the Diagnostic and Statistical Manual of Mental Disorders). The DSM is used by professionals to diagnose the disorder.

Later on in the book, we will share the lived experience of some of the symptoms of the disorder. It is also important to recognize the disorder from the medical perspective, and therefore we have included the symptoms from a medical professional perspective.

- Emotional instability and mood swings including intense, episodic emotional anguish, irritability, and anxiety attacks, or panic attacks

- Anger that is inappropriate, intense, and difficult to control

- Chronic feelings of emptiness

- Impulsive and self-damaging acts such as excessive spending, unsafe and inappropriate sexual conduct, substance abuse, reckless driving, and binge eating

- Recurrent suicidal ideation, behaviour, gestures, and threats, or self-harming

- A marked and persistent unstable self-image or sense of identity

- Suspicious episodes, and even paranoid ideation, or transient and stress related dissociation.

- Intense fear of abandonment, and frantic efforts to avoid real or imagined abandonment

- A pattern of intense, unstable relationships

It is common for Borderline to be misdiagnosed and for diagnosis to occur years after the first occurrence of the symptoms. The disorder commonly co-occurs, or masks itself as other disorders, and late diagnosis or misdiagnosis can exacerbate the problem.

What are the possible causes?

THE CAUSE OF BORDERLINE Personality Disorder and other personality disorders are not fully understood, but it is generally accepted that the environment plays a role in personality development, and that parenting contributes to attachment style which is key in relationships.

Consequently, it is found that the disorder can be brought on by childhood abuse and childhood neglect.

A genetic pre-disposition of the disorder, shown in family history, can also increase the risk. And some research has shown brain abnormalities in people with the disorder.

What is the Available Treatment?

BORDERLINE PERSONALITY Disorder seems surrounded by myths of incurability and hopelessness, but these *are* myths.

Some experts are dedicated to providing the support that people with Borderline Personality Disorder need. The treatment recommendations are also likely to change and improve as minds open and stigma reduces. Educating oneself and researching the views and recommendations of experts in the field can go a long way in providing a better understanding, and importantly hope.

Not every therapist and psychiatrist is suitable to work with people with Borderline Personality Disorder. Selecting experts who are suitably qualified and experienced with this disorder can be the defining factor in successful treatment. Finding the right match and synergy with each other can lead to success. Patients have a bad reputation for not sticking with treatment. However, this may be the result of the under-estimated importance for people with this disorder to find the right therapist. Encouragement to seek out the correct (as in the correctly matched) therapist can lead to successful long-term treatment and results.

In addition to some of the treatment described briefly below, it is worth mentioning that exercise, a healthy diet, and general coping skills go a long way in helping when they are built into a routine. Therapists also suggest journaling and art as other forms of healthy release for the build-up of intensity that occurs with the disorder.

Psychotherapy is the primary form of treatment

PSYCHOTHERAPY SEEMS to be the most effective form of treatment and supports any other treatment's success. A team approach including a psychiatrist is recommended by some experts.

With long term consistent therapy some psychologists report significant improvement in their patients. There are psychologists who specialize in personality disorders. These experts who have relevant experience with clients with Borderline Personality Disorder, and who report success with their patients, are worth seeking out.

The main problems with Borderline Personality Disorder are deep issues that require consistent work in a safe space such as with a trusted therapist. The outward reactions (described in some of the symptoms) may result from unhelpful internal beliefs and fears caused by underlying childhood trauma. Long term therapy provides the opportunity to meaningfully address this underlying trauma in the context of the individual's present real-life triggers, and practical struggles. It provides a safe space in which beliefs and fears can be challenged and explored.

Borderline Personality Disorder is complex, professionals have differing views, and there is often a stigma associated with the disorder. Selecting the right therapist can, therefore, be important. A therapist who has hope and the belief that those with the disorder can lead healthier and happier lives with more fulfilling relationships will work with their patients to improve.

As mentioned, the disorder can co-occur with other problems, and it will subsequently be easier for someone with relevant experience to successfully identify and treat Borderline Personality Disorder.

What is DBT (Dialectical Behaviour Therapy) and Mindfulness?

DIALECTICAL BEHAVIORAL Therapy uses Mindfulness, Distress Tolerance, Interpersonal Effectiveness, and Emotional Regulation skills to attempt to improve behavioral responses to change and stress. It is commonly used as a component of the treatment of people with Borderline Personality Disorder.

A key strength of DBT is known to be its Mindfulness component which focuses on being in the moment. Mindfulness can help one to calm down in times of crisis and to consequently avoid going into an automatic negative response when triggered. It can help a person to engage in useful coping strategies during times of acute stress. The resulting pause between action and impulse can reduce suicidal and other destructive behaviors. As such, DBT can prove to be helpful in reducing some of the symptoms of the disorder.

Is there medication for Borderline Personality Disorder?

ALTHOUGH PSYCHIATRISTS and medication can be helpful, there is no specific medication that can cure the disorder on its own. However, medication does appear to be successful in reducing some of the symptoms of the disorder and is also known to help treat some of the co-occurring emotional disorders, such as anxiety and depression.

An integrated team approach including medication is backed up by the logic that the cause of Borderline Personality Disorder is partly genetic and partly environmental. It follows that help in both areas could be required. Again, a professional who has experience and skill with Borderline Personality Disorder treatment is required.

A team approach enables therapy and medication to take appropriate roles at appropriate times in the treatment plan to support the overall goal of well-being. When symptoms are highly destructive, medication can be the help required to stabilize. When therapy is established, which can take time to start taking effect, medication may be called upon during periods of crisis only, such as in the case of a major depressive episode. Team support, that consists of professionals who have skills and experience with treating this disorder, can help to guide an individual to the correct decisions for them.

Chapter 2: What is it like to live with Borderline Personality Disorder?

This morning I felt really bad and needed a friend, but I didn't know what was appropriate or not, so I gave up on the friend option, and prayed for God to hold me. And then a great friend messaged me! I could hardly believe how quickly I went from feeling hopeless to feeling blessed. Can you blame me, given this situation? God held me - I am blessed!

Mood swings

I OFTEN SWING FROM feeling hopeless to feeling grateful. My tears transform while they are falling. They can leave my eyes with bitter loneliness, and by the time they reach my lips they are sweet gratitude. They feel like iridescent rainbows streaming down my face. My mother used to say that as a child I would cry and laugh at the same time. I have no shortage of emotion, and my true colors feel like all the colors!

The field of Gray

"Out beyond ideas of wrongdoing and right-doing, there is a field. I'll meet you there."

~ Rumi

THERE ARE MOMENTS WHEN I truly wonder if I am cursed or blessed. The truth is, I think, somewhere in between – I am both, yet neither. Imagine, if you will, a field of tiny black and white blades of grass. Each of them is black, or white. But when you look at the whole field from a distance, you see the big picture which is a large gray field – neither black nor white, just gray.

Maybe black and white do not exist, except as parts of the reality of gray. A tough one for someone like me, but I came up with that to try to understand why it *seemed* black and white. I tend to get lost inside situations where my mind goes black or white. In that moment when a friend cancels an appointment, or if a text awaits a reply for hours, it can *seem* like I am unloved by that person, and like that relationship is a mistake.

Love and hate

BUT IT'S JUST A MOMENT of madness. I do not hate the person. How could I hate someone I love? I cannot, contrary to popular belief, but also contrary to my own angry words at extreme times. I can run away and keep my distance if my BPD gets triggered. I can become insecure, but I still love them. I don't swing from love to hate. I swing from secure to insecure. The love is constant.

Letting go

I HAVE DEEP ISSUES letting go. Attachment is a major theme in my life. The bright side of this is that I will not let go of a relationship impulsively. I am not a likely candidate to be abandoning anyone without significant thought and reflection first. But, I am a likely candidate to do so if I am convinced they are going to dump me. When I feel that someone wants to walk away but isn't finding the courage to take that step – yes, then I will take it boldly. I could be wrong. Maybe they didn't intend walking away, and I just imagined it out of my insecurities. This possibility could lead me to question my decision and try to make it work again, which could lead to getting back together. I am usually the one getting rejected – Oh – wait, am I?

Real or Perceived Rejection?

I AM USUALLY THE ONE *feeling* like I am the one being rejected. This perceived rejection is a major problem. I think it's a key issue for you to be aware of because my awareness of this fades or disappears entirely when I'm triggered. If you are not rejecting your person with BPD, you may need to clearly point that out. You could be misunderstood by a tainted BPD lens. I have just done it while writing to you – thinking my pattern is not to reject, but actually...

I do leave when I think I am going to be left – there – I said it. That is extremely hard for me to say, and it almost rings untrue because of my abandonment issues. It is such a deep issue that sits at the core of my BPD. More communication, around this, from my significant other will be appreciated. Your presence of mind on this for us (our relationship) will be appreciated because it can be a stubborn blind spot to me. I do not want to not see it, I CAN'T see it. I'm trying. Can you see it for us in these times?

I am trying to admit my reality here. I am trying not to look at our relationship through my tainted lens. I am trying to let you into my world. But don't turn that against me, please. Don't look back at me through my tainted lens either – try not to too. This is my kryptonite, and if you throw it at me, I will act out at you. Now, you may think that is a threat or manipulation – it's not – it's my honesty.

Now I'm vulnerable. Please resist saying, "It's because you have BPD. You are blind." Would you tell a blind person to see? You would maybe move something out of her way, or take her hand to guide her, or give her a cane. A blind man can still not lead a blind man. In times of arguments, I hope you will not fall into this hole with me. It is not just for me, but for us. If you can appreciate that it will be in our best interest to try to help me see the reality in these times, then you may agree that it is not selfish for me to call on your support with this trigger. I know this isn't easy for you because no one wants to be rejected. I understand that it is a trigger for everyone else too. I am trying to learn to step back and look at the whole field, and not that one little dangerously pitch-black blade. But I don't have it all figured out yet.

Complex lashing out and hard goodbyes

I THOUGHT I CALLED my ex to ask his opinion on a project I'm working on. I didn't mean to have an outburst at him. When I thought about it afterward, I tried to piece the puzzle together. I know I'll be living alone again soon, and when I do live alone, my ex tends to want to get back together. I don't want that cycle of our destructive relationship to start again. I can't afford another 5 years of that. But I didn't realize that was what I was trying to say. And I don't have a clue as to why I didn't say it directly or consciously. If I did, I doubt he would have taken it on-board anyway.

So maybe, sub-consciously, I was trying to make him hate me, so that he does not come back to hurt me. I only realized that I was being unreasonable after the ten texts I sent him. I was sorry. I didn't really wish I never met him. I do love him, but I don't want us to be together because I hate the way he makes me feel. I feel like I would be vulnerable if he returned to me because I don't know if I would have the presence of mind to say, "No". My attachment to him would kick in, and I could make an unwise decision.

Intense family bonds and bound-errries

I KNOW IT'S YOUR LIFE, and I don't have the right to interfere in the way you run it. But the way you gave me the silent treatment for months, even though it was my fault, shakes my trust in our relationship. I know you love me, but I do not know if I trust you. I feel emotionally unsafe around you now. And saying this is just too inappropriate – I can sense that on another level, so I just stay away week after week.

I was trying not to interfere in your life, but I do have strong feelings about the people I am close to. I'd kept those thoughts inside me for a decade, knowing that it was not appropriate for me to share my opinion on how you raise your child. Was it really your child I was defending? Or does the way you raise your child trigger issues in me over the way I was raised? Sometimes I am confused about whether I am right or wrong, and about whether I agree or disagree with my actions!

When I am in a triggered state, it's not easy to keep quiet. I'd been through a relationship breakup, and I was fragile when I exploded. Then later on I questioned what I said. I've been thinking about it for 4 months now, and I can't count how many different perspectives I've had on it. When have you stopped thinking about it? My logic says you probably didn't waste much time on it.

I feel like I love you too much, and I worry often about interfering as a result of our closeness. This worry leads me to stay too far away from you. It's because I care about your life and your happiness. I don't want to get between you and your partner. I don't want to interfere with how you raise your kids. But if I keep extra quiet, it builds up to eventually explode once a decade. I hate this about the way I am.

If I love you wrongly, that would be harmful, and love is not supposed to be harmful. God knows I feel harmed by how others controlled my life, and I don't want to do that to you, in any way at all, ever.

Sometimes you do things that affect me too, but I am too afraid to accept that I do not like it, or to speak out about it because I second guess my judgment. To question my own judgment is an unstable, shaky, shifting place to be in, and it feels unsettling. You matter to me. Your happiness is important to me, and I'm trying to do what's right.

But my integrity is important to me too, so I do sometimes say what I think is right, even if it crosses a boundary. The problem is that I do not always know what is right. I wish I did.

When it comes to perceptions of BPD, this is ironic – I feel like I walk on eggshells, watching that I don't say the wrong things. I feel so judged, and I feel like such a misfit that I think I will say the wrong thing. And that is usually a recipe for an explosion. Where does that leave me? Isolated and alone much of the time. Alone because I want to protect those I love from me. Do I need to feel this way?

Resolving Issues

MY RELATIONSHIPS SUFFER when things are left unresolved. This is possibly because my experiences with my parents were left unresolved since childhood. Some people tend to want space, and then come back and start again. But to me, nothing is resolved this way, and by then I have made assumptions that they either love me less, have punished me, or whatever other sometimes convoluted way I find of making sense of the issue.

The issue needs to be resolved in order for it to be processed on my side. Otherwise, I carry around all these unprocessed issues. I attach them to existing core baggage which becomes heavier, and which threatens to resurface all the more. Then the fear of pending explosion makes me anxious, and anxiety eventually explodes.

It may seem like I make a mountain out of a molehill, and from your perspective maybe that's true. But from my perspective, there is something beneath that iceberg's peak that I feel should be resolved. Resolution is important to me in maintaining good relationships and moving forward. It helps me avoid my unhealthy tendency to isolate or push others away. I am referring here to significantly close personal relationships, and not to people who are at a distance.

A safe space

HEALTHY RELATIONSHIPS in my life have a safe space. It's either always been that way, has naturally developed, or is being consciously created. It can come after an outburst when the need for space becomes evident. A safe space means I can say yes or no, and so can the other person. A safe space means we understand that neither of us is perfect. A safe space means that the other person realizes that I have some differences and am unusually intense, and together we try to define how to deal with that intensity in terms of our relationship. If and when this happens, I realize that this person truly accepts me, or wants me in their life.

When someone is telling me they have a problem with the way I have behaved in our relations with each other, and that they want a better way to relate with me, then I hear that I need to work at things. But I also hear that I am wanted in that person's life. This is useful feedback for me. If I respond to this, or if I initiate this conversation with you, then to me that means we are realizing we are welcome in each other's lives, but that we need to draw certain boundaries to make the relationship healthier.

Social anxiety

I WAS AT A SCHOOL CONCERT the other evening, and I recognized someone I used to work with about 6 years ago. We were never friends, but I did like her quite a lot. I admired her. I walked up to her in the corridor at the concert, and I hugged her. She looked shocked. We chatted for a minute, and then I turned around and walked away, realizing I was getting in the way of everyone focusing on finding their children. I am not always this socially awkward. It's a new thing for me. I had to have a glass of wine to get over my embarrassment of what she must think of me gushing up to her like that and violating her personal space. Am I touch-deprived, or just socially anxious these days? Should

I hide more, or is that the problem? Social anxiety is a fairly new problem I have. I am trying not to worry anyone with my chaos, but as a result, I've now become a recluse. Where is the middle, please?

I feel tired

I GET TIRED FROM MY efforts at trying to be a reasonable human being. I am aware that my reactions are sometimes intense. I try to manage them, but trying makes me tired. And being tired makes me more easily triggered. So, it's a cycle. I tend to need more rest than I feel is reasonable. I wouldn't openly admit that to people because that would sound unreasonable or lazy. I suspect an unreasonable mind may need some unreasonable care to make things reasonable!

I should probably create more routine in life. My lack of routine stresses me out. I tend to have to think about everything all the time because I haven't planned out a routine. In this way, I manifest more chaos.

I am on high alert much of the time which makes me feel tired. Finding ways to operate on a healthy auto-pilot may help me. I get scared to fall into habits in case they become bad habits. In jobs in my past, I have fallen deeply into environments where I would lose a year at a time by focusing too much on just one thing. I feel like I am damned if I do, and damned if I don't. The balancing act needs practice and commitment to self-awareness.

My state and my environment

MUCH OF WHAT I'VE SHARED so far is me in a vulnerable state. In other states, I can take more than seems humanly possible. I can be the last man standing in a team effort, or the only one who can deal with a difficult boss.

My state of mind is usually affected by an emotional relationship trigger such as rejection or abuse. Once I'm badly triggered and unable to resolve an issue, signs of my inner state become visible in my environment. I notice that this is particularly true as I get older. I seem to have less capacity or will to hide my real state. Of course, I would ultimately like to improve my state, but hiding it superficially is becoming less possible. Perhaps it is an extreme expression of integrity where the outside has to match the inside. I do not pretend easily, but I used to try to be more acceptable outwardly when I was younger. Still, I know it would be useful if I could try the outside-in approach with myself. I wish I could push myself in the right direction with these relatively simple things.

If I were to let you close enough, you would notice that when I am stable, I dress confidently and comfortably, and the house is clean. I'm not a tidy person, but certain spaces like tabletops and counters will always be clear when I am in a healthy state. There may be some flowers in a vase, and the windows will all be wide open.

When, on the other hand, I am dealing with something and struggling to find clarity within, then my environment suffers and reflects my inward state. I will not get to the dishes, and the countertops and tables can stay in chaotic states for weeks. Curtains can remain closed for entire days, and the doors can remain locked for days.

A self-care thing for me would be to regularly manage my environment in order to shift my inner state. I do find that shakes me out of things, yet I tend to favor going from inside to out which takes too long. If I lived with someone who had BPD, I would watch for outer signs. I would initiative an improvement in the outer to encourage the inner shift. My examples are unique to me, but the concept can be shared. If you see something in the environment that is unhealthy or out of the ordinary, it can be a sign of a change on the inside.

When I am stable, I eat because I am hungry, I try to go the healthy route, and I enjoy my food. When I am unstable, I eat to fill a void, to distract me from my pain, and just because I do not feel okay. I eat too much, yet do not enjoy the food. When I was younger, I would eat too little as a coping mechanism.

Managing my state is crucial, and on a practical level there is much I could do that I seem to not consider most days. If I do not want to engage in a conversation or event because of my state, I am probably best left alone. Yet there are times when I am unable to manage my state for a long period, and then I opt for disengaging from most people which ultimately leads to relationships fading. It is such a complex place inside my head. It feels like it is.

Does that give you an idea of how my way of thinking is? Is it different from yours? I "know" everyone is looking at me wondering what goes on in my head, and why after 5 years in a relationship I still can't see what they spotted a few months in. But I am assuming, aren't I? And this is exactly what I think the problem is. I cannot and should not assume to know what you are thinking, or why you are doing what you do. And you should not assume to know why I am doing things either. Because you just don't know what goes on inside me.

You may see some of what I do, but let's be clear that you do not know the why. You're welcome to research BPD which could help, and you're welcome to ask me which could help. Sometimes, however, even I don't know why until later because I tend to be impulsive. But not always – it depends on my state of mind. At the moment I am fragile, so any little thing can trigger me into an inappropriate response. Then I get that embarrassing feeling of when you wake up the next morning remembering what you did while drunk. I wasn't drunk, but this is the feeling. Sometimes I get drunk on my disorder if I am in an unstable state. And the more I stare at the steps in front of me trying not to trip over them, the more I do trip over them.

Unpacking the reality of some symptoms

"I am not like most people. I do things that normal people wouldn't do. But don't judge me just because you don't get me"
~ K. Marie

Abandonment and Trust

YOU PROBABLY KNOW THAT I have deep-seated core fears of abandonment. This creates trust issues that lead me to trust only (or mostly only) myself, ironically especially in times of being triggered. Making my own decisions is important. I do not enjoy being told what to do. That is another catch 22 because when I'm triggered my thinking is flawed, and trusting my gut becomes unknowingly trusting my insecurities, leading to errors. Having someone or something external to turn to for advice in times like this is needed. Yet, I struggle to reach out. I do not want to be a burden, and I don't know who to trust. The stigma scares me – what will they think of me?

I turn to my spiritual side of life where I ask for guidance. And I also found a safe place for some advice online where I watch videos by experts in the field who I find helpful. It is not easy to find experts who I trust around BPD, and the few I found are priceless to me. They put out useful information that's labeled appropriately, and that's available for me to watch or listen to when I need it without having to feel I am disturbing or burdening them. This way I feel I get support from a *real* person who does care about people like me, and who has a sense of understanding and education about people with BPD. It is also easy to trust someone I do not know as my trust is based on their sound judgment, and not on the relationship with them. I can hear how this sounds counter-intuitive, but because I struggle with relationships using remote online resources takes the relationship hassle out of it.

I listen to mature therapists, coaches, or experts who come from a sense of hope, care, honesty, and respectful concern for both me and others I am involved with. Education on BPD has been important to me. Supportive videos with information, skills, and tools, have been useful. I also follow select relationship coaches online because much of my instability involves relationships. I am so grateful for these people online – they make a difference to the world.

I do not know if it is because of my diagnosis, but I feel a sense of being an unpopular patient with therapists face to face. Maybe I am just too complicated? If I had support, I would definitely appreciate my loved ones making these appointments for me, so that therapists would take me more seriously.

Event with Abandonment Trigger

HERE IS WHAT IT FELT like for me when I was badly triggered by fear of abandonment.

I was in an intense romantic relationship. It was a passionate relationship with much fighting and much loving. We laughed much, and we cried much. One day we argued. I don't remember what it was about. Everything happened very fast. He walked out very upset, and red in the face. I couldn't believe it was happening to me again. My thoughts were racing as was my heart. I was in a loop that went like this:

"Why does everybody leave?

No one loves me.

I can't believe he left me.

I can't believe this is happening.

This is really happening. I am alone again.

Everyone leaves.

Everyone just leaves.

Everyone leaves."

I was distraught. I was panicked. I reached up to the cupboard where the painkillers were. I took them out, and just kept pouring them into my hand. All the while that loop kept playing in my mind. All I could hear, think, and feel was that everyone leaves. I kept saying that he is gone, and that everyone leaves me. And I kept taking the pills.

Then I walked outside the door, and stood outside for a second to try to breathe. Taking the pills felt like a release for the impossible intensity of the pain of rejection. And then, out of nowhere, there *he* was standing in front of me. I struggled. I couldn't make sense of that moment. I believed he LEFT me for good. I didn't know how to deal with his return because it didn't make sense with my version of reality. I asked him what he was doing there, and I asked in loud abusive language. I just didn't understand what he was doing back there if he had left me.

Then it registered that I'd taken an overdose of pills, and I started thinking about my life and everyone else that I loved. I got my car keys and decided I was going to go to the hospital to get myself "saved" from my momentary insanity. There he was standing in front of the car, not knowing what I'd done, he was trying to stop me from driving off. I screamed at him, telling him to get out of there because he had left me, and I drove myself to the hospital.

The next morning, I was groggy and staring out the window when it all started coming back to me. For the first time, I remembered things that I blocked out entirely during the event. I played the whole thing back in my mind trying to understand what happened. And then it came to me – I saw his passport on the dresser and his cell phone on the table. He is a foreigner and would never leave without his passport.

How did I believe that he left for good when I saw his passport with my own eyes? And his cell phone was there too! It turned out he was not a ghost at all, but I had fooled myself because my beliefs about everyone leaving were so strong that I simply would not believe any evidence to the contrary. He didn't leave me! He was only gone outside for a walk to cool off after the argument. He was doing the right thing to prevent himself from becoming aggressive. I was shocked at the reality I was discovering about the destructive power of my beliefs. I was shocked at how deceptive the mind can be. At the same time, I was relieved about the discovery. This event was when I was 30 years old.

I had been through experiences in my twenties where I would wake up the next morning not knowing why I'd been so upset. I would have to just move on with life, with no explanation, no understanding, and no sense made of what happened.

At 35, I got into a depressed state, and I took an overdose again in a destructive impulsive attempt to end the pain. I called a friend to help me, and I got help at a hospital. That was the last time I self-harmed so directly. I do not see either of these events as suicide attempts, but as moments of lapse in judgment from my mental illness. They were impulsive actions that I regretted, and that I got help for.

I hope you are not judging me for this. In both cases I was not looking for attention, but was wanting to escape the pain. But these actions obviously led to more problems. I hope this will never happen again, but I do fear it because I don't want to take my life.

I despise the stigma around suicide, and I will tell you a story about the stigma a little later. But for now, let's talk about something less upsetting! Time for a cup of tea. I will try to keep it a little lighter now, okay? I don't want to be too much for you as we walk on this journey.

Pace yourself – take a break if you need to. This will be here for you when you're up to carrying on with me ☺ And thank you, for reading this, and for trying to make sense of the chaos with me. It is going to feel better when we understand things better, and it will come together.

The brighter side

"I am a believer that no one is perfect, and that everyone is perfect."

HOW ABOUT A FEW LITTLE analogies to the brighter side of BPD?

Do you like roses? Sometimes I see us as roses. People in general, but yes those of us with BPD especially. There is a legend, you see, that roses developed thorns because they were so sweet that the entire rose bush would get eaten up by animals. It needed protection. Roses are sweet. I am a believer that no one is perfect, and that everyone is perfect. I would love to be loved like a rose, to be appreciated for my sweet delicateness, and for my thorns to be watched out for as carefully as possible. They are not meant to be hurting anyone. But I don't want someone to throw me out entirely because of my thorns. And I don't want to throw myself out because of those thorns either.

What about those gorgeous VW beetles? I love those flower-power kinds of buggies. But once in a while, you see one stuck on the side of the road! In these times, when you see someone with a car like that, there is only one reason they drive that car – they truly love it! They find it special, quirky, attractive, cute, full of Herbie drama, personality, and love. And if... okay, *when* it gets stuck on the side of the road they will get it home, find the problem, and start again. Maybe it just needs a rest, and it will be back soon! This is the way I want to be loved. Because I do want to be myself, like Herbie, like everyone wants to be. Yes, I need to fix myself up, and I'm trying, but I also want to be me.

Feeling calmer? Can we get back to some serious business? You know I am serious and interested in things deeply. But I am aware that I can be too much, and I do make an effort to chuck myself into more reasonable waters for the sake of those around me – if anyone is listening ☺ I hope you are now, so I am trying for you, okay ☺ I want to engage with you. I don't want you to run. Stay awhile, but at your own pace, okay?

Unexpected emotional turmoil for no apparent reason

AGAIN, IT ALL DEPENDS on the state I am generally in. My moods can change more rapidly than even I thought was possible. I could be in a good mood trying to focus on work for two hours, and then find myself holding onto a wall with tears flooding my face because I feel sad. This outburst, if I am alone, can be a good release of the sadness. But if I am not alone it can be a drawn-out and counter-productive process. Firstly, I will try not to have the outburst if I'm not alone. If I do it will affect those around me. Then there will be awkwardness and guilt. If I have someone with me, they will be disturbed from what they're doing, and will (hopefully) come and hug me, which I will really appreciate. Or they will complain (hopefully not), and I will feel offended, and that could lead to a fight.

If they complain or roll their eyes at me when I am dealing with an influx of internal turmoil, I feel unseen. They could think I am pretending, and I know I am not. But because I know they're doubting me, I could doubt myself too. I know I'm not doing it for attention because I am feeling the same way when I am all alone, and most days nobody knows about these outbursts of emotion.

They start thinking I overreact, waste time, or am just out of reality. They do not realize that in my reality there is a storm on the inside, and if I do not manage to get that storm out of me in one way, it will get out of me in another way. I think crying is probably one of my healthiest and safest outlets, and I want to create more alone space and time in my life, so I can just cry when I need to. Holding onto emotions and "behaving" for everyone else leaves me with a tank ready to explode at any moment. I do not want to explode onto others or implode either.

I am ≠ BPD

"I despise my own hypersensitiveness, which requires so much reassurance. It is certainly abnormal to crave so much to be loved and understood."
-Anaïs Nin

I WANT TO TALK ABOUT this issue of identifying me with my personality disorder. The stigma out there tells people who I am. But the media and far-removed people do not personally know me, do they? I have come to believe that "me" and my personality are two different things. I know a lady who is harsh towards others in her outer personality. She is coldly distant, and seems unapproachable. I spent some years around this lady. I have come to know that she is one of the most caring individuals I've met. What lies inside the heart is not always there for the world to see, but in a long-term relationship, you do see the character of a person as you experience them in their fullness.

I may at times be looking at myself and others through a broken lens, but I do not think it is helpful for the other to look back at me through that same lens. See the real person, and assess reality which is in all likelihood – yep, gray. My personality is broken. My humanity is whole. We are all flawed, and we are all intrinsically beautiful. If you love someone for who they are, then you tend to want them around for their essence, and not for the personality that it is all wrapped up in.

At the end of the day, the wrapping may get in your way, be wrinkled, old, greasy, troublesome, whatever – but just beneath the surface lies a real person. We are all unique, we are all here for a reason in my view, and we are all in this together with those we choose to surround ourselves with. In my eyes, personality is just another level of the skin. It is not equal to me. Yes, I must try to take better care of it, and to better use it in my interactions. But my BPD lens must not be what I always see life through, and it must not be what you always look back at me through either. If we keep that going, neither of us will be seen for who we really are, and there will be no depth to our relationship.

I try to let my character direct my personality. I don't always succeed, but this is what it looks like when I'm trying. I have an ex-husband. He was my best friend and my trusted other for a decade. When I am in crisis my mind goes straight to him. His phone number is at my fingertips, and his arms are in my daydreams. But I tell myself to shake it off for the precise reason that I do love and care for him. I must keep no contact with him because we are through with that relationship, and he has moved on. Of course, I feel the pull stronger than most because I have BPD. I imagine things in vivid detail. I miss his comfort, and I long for it at times. But, what I think is my character switches it off knowing that I do not want to cause any pain in his world. I try to stop thinking about him, and hardly mention his name (even in my own head) because I need to shut it out in order to survive without harming him by making contact.

Identity crises

> *"It will take an appreciation of my inner journey to understand whether this one who wanders is indeed lost."*

THERE IS ANOTHER PROBLEM with my so-called personality, and this is the paradox of creating better behavior, habits, and perspectives. The introspection that BPD recovery and management requires of me has been slowly disintegrating the self I was, and is recreating newer and newer versions of me. This feeds into, or is an identity disturbance because it disturbs my stability. Yet, depending on my perspective, I sometimes call this growth.

The changing self in BPD can be very unhealthy when that self becomes enmeshed and attached to the identity of others. But if the changing self is a result of attempts to improve behaviors and unhealthy attachments, then can it be a healthy changing self? This is my personal perspective, and nothing to do with expert opinion. It will take an appreciation of my inner journey to understand whether this one who wanders is indeed lost.

The outer reality is not always a sign of illness. It can also be a sign of healing. I personally feel that my spiritual journey and my mental illness have a thin line between them. It is challenging to get to know this line. Personally, there are times I have to remind myself that I am living in an insane world full of greed, war, and strife. The fact that I am not okay sometimes makes me feel sane because walking around like everything is okay in an utter war zone does not sound normal to me. But yes, I get it, I do need to make this life work better for me and for us, even though it is far from sane.

Attachments and blurred lines between me and others

I HAVE COME TO REALIZE that in my relationships with people I am close to, I sometimes blurred the lines between them and me. When I recognized this, I made a strong and painful attempt to tear myself away from them, and to put some distance between us. Space is healthy. But I don't know how much distance is enough. There are times when I feel I have to detach myself in certain ways for the other person's benefit. I do want that person – those people – you – to be unhappy, and I do not want to stifle anyone. I struggle with drawing lines and finding the right distance, so sometimes I opt for less because I do not want to harm. And sometimes it still harms. I hope this is not as hard for the other person to deal with it as it is for me.

I have said things out of turn because I am intense, and because I notice subtle situations that others do not. An example of this may be someone feeling emotionally humiliated by others, or someone feeling embarrassed and put down by others' seemingly harmless banter. I can sense the unspoken pain from those who are sensitive. Sometimes I feel like an idiot about what I sense because I know others will say there is no evidence for what I feel. Research shows that people with BPD do sense the unspoken signals of negative things, and do have generally high empathy. However, research also shows that this is skewed towards the negative side, so we may miss the positive signs. Add to that insecurities and state of being, and it becomes yet another challenge. This is really quite confusing for me. Empathy and intuition are sort of like faith – one doesn't want to question it, but intuition, gut feelings, and insecurities can get mixed up.

I have stories of intuitive experiences that reflect my strong intuitive sense – it is off-topic to mention it here, but it adds context for my point. I can only hope I'm wrong about the negative things I feel I witness. For reality's sake, I hope the BPD is exaggerating things. But the jury is out on that one! Intuition is a tough one to prove or disprove, and I do not want to fight that battle. I personally value my intuition, but in order to trust it fully, I have to be able to manage my state of being better. Ah, the complexities!

Stress Intolerance, and are you tired?

NOW THAT WE HAVE TALKED through relationships, I am pretty exhausted. And I guess this is an important admission. I tend to be deep, complicated, or serious. Maybe it is not depth. Maybe it is convoluted immaturity – you decide. In either case, I sense that I tire people out. They do not have to say it. I tire myself out too after a long think with myself, or after a deep conversation with myself or another. So, self-care here, for you, is space from me! We all need space.

If you do find something beautiful in this relationship, that is great – it could be intensely sweet musical notes, but like any composition, there are spaces of silence in between that make those notes meaningful. I have failed to provide suitable space in some of my relationships. I want to create, accept, welcome, and nurture those spaces apart. It is tempting to want to reject those spaces – tempting for you too perhaps. If you are in a romantic relationship with someone so passionate and intense then space can seem ridiculous. But if you want that passion to stay sweet, space is a marvelous cushion.

I really do not know how I managed to go through life up to this point with as little space as I've had. Now that I've discovered that space and silence have a beautiful way of absorbing the overflow, and of helping to process, I find it vital. It is vital for my relationship with myself too. I just have to watch that I don't isolate.

Stress contributes to the state of mind, and because I am already having to feel such a lot of intensity from how I operate, stress has a heightened effect on me. When I was a child, my stress tolerance was high and pushed to limits. I was a happy child amid chaos. We are built to survive this way. But as an adult, it irks me when I sense the way people think I am weak and have a low tolerance. And I am weak, and I do have a low tolerance. The slightest thing can stress me out.

The more something means to me, the more I can stress about it. A party in honor of someone, for example. This used to be a big deal for me because it's an opportunity to show someone how much they are appreciated and valued. This used to be a joy for me, but I have put myself under so much pressure with the meaning I've added to this one, that I exhaust myself. I sabotage, leaving gift shopping for the last minute, and then rushing, or not settling for an option until I have considered every other possible option. I am not one for malls and shopping on any day. I have developed so much anxiety around this that there are times when I just give up, get sick, and don't even show up to see the person. When I have a significant other, I am more likely to cope with these sorts of pressures because then I would ask advice or company. My ex-partner used to come shopping with me sometimes, only because he saw how much I stressed, and the support of his presence meant the world to me. I feel guilty that

I need someone to help me get through that, so I need to just accept that I can do it or not do it – alone. If I don't do it, the guilt that comes with that is heavy, and it takes me a long time to get over it.

I self-sabotage and create stress in various ways. With my work, I attract big or different jobs. I don't regret that entirely because boredom is worse than a challenge to me. I tend to not know where the impossible line is, and I'll always try to make things happen. This has led me to work for nights on end, neglecting the perspective of life as a whole, and compromising myself and my relationships because I can get so intensely involved in my experience of one thing. It's that black and white thinking. Success at work tends to mean failure at something else, and failure at work tends to mean time for something else. But I need both, of course, success at work, and the rest of life. You know this already. I need to consciously remind myself, or I could get stuck in my focused mindset where I forget about everything else. Can you see how this could be a strength? I can see how this could be, and I envy those who have mastered that focus. To me, it remains a weakness!

I liked it when my partner used to come to say, "Hey, let's go to bed." I wouldn't know when the time to stop is. Giving up and letting go, or stopping at good enough is something many people do easily. But for some, how to give up and let go is a strength we need to learn. With my BPD I hold onto things – impossible deadlines and projects, dead-end relationships, and a line of empty shampoo bottles in my shower! That last bit of letting go, throwing out, saying we're done, saying we give up, saying it's over, saying it's impossible, saying it's finished, is tough!

Not giving up does not always lead to success. It can be a recipe for failure too.

"With my BPD I hold onto things – impossible deadlines and projects, dead-end relationships, and a line of empty shampoo bottles in my shower!"

Feeling disabled

I HAVE OFTEN FELT LIKE I am living with a disability. I've been depressed to the point of debilitation, I've stayed in bed for days, I've been unable to open the curtains and let in the light, I've been unable to speak from being triggered, I've been unable to answer the phone, I have been disabled and incapacitated.

I have been ashamed to say I am disabled. Ashamed because I felt others would only see my weakness. I have been strong in all that I had to endure in my journey too, but people don't see that easily. Vulnerability is mistaken for weakness. I am also afraid of what people will do if they see my disability – if I show up with it on my sleeve. I don't like the way society treats those who are physically disabled. Much of society does not accept these fellow human beings as equals – they are sometimes shoved into a corner somewhere to live out their days away from those they love and away from broader experiences of life. This scares me to death. I identify with these people strongly. I feel empathy for them, and I wish I had the strength to contribute to solving their problem in society.

Why would I want to entrust my state of well-being to the society that does this to the vulnerable? When society disrespects these people by giving them more limited options than others, to education and to all the rest, and when society discards these people, that says a lot about the way society treats people who are seen as different. We are all unique. But I can hardly blame us for not showing up for help, support, or coming out with our various differences when this is what we see in the world.

As someone living with BPD, I have felt at times that I have lost my childhood. Freedom in my adulthood is subsequently seriously important to me. I do want help with my illness, but it has got to be my choice and my decision. There is only one time that I want someone else to decide – and that is when I'm unsafe, as in suicidal, then I want help even if I will disagree! Please do not leave me for dead then, or you help me prove the lies to be true – the lies that nobody cares. I do not find it easy to reach out. And if I reach out to you, you may be the only one I reach out to. This is not to manipulate you into any relationship with me. When I say help, I mean help. I do not mean attach to me, nor stay with me. If you cannot handle it, that's okay. Drive me to an ER, and leave me there, or call someone who you know cares about me, or call an ambulance, and then walk away.

But when I feel that bad in your presence from a trigger in our relationship, and you walk away, I may die. This has happened to others, and no one listened because they thought it was manipulation – it was not. It was an impulsive attempt to escape the pain. Illness requires respect and help. Would you walk away from someone bleeding on the street? Why then would you walk away from me when I am emotionally bleeding on your floor, unable to speak, hiding under your bed out of being triggered into a state that is clearly not normal? See this for what it is, please, and then run if that's what you want to do! I do not want to be embarrassed and ashamed, but I will take that if it keeps me alive. No one wants to die from falling accidentally. They would prefer if someone, anyone, called them an ambulance. And yet, people who claim to care, walk away claiming this is manipulation. People's lives are at stake. You can always leave a relationship, and that isn't my point. A suicide threat from someone with BPD, or from anyone, should be taken seriously. It means one is at risk, and it calls for action. At this stage, one needs help to take action in getting support. Suicidal people are not okay.

Unfortunately, because relationships are a major trigger in BPD, it is complicated when someone is suicidal because of an issue in the relationship. Here especially, perspective is needed from the other person. Perspective that maybe the relationship is over, but a person's life does not also have to be over.

Chapter 3: How to understand and support me

Not reaching out to a friend

I told you before that when I need a friend, I am not so good at reaching out, so sometimes you may feel I'm closed to you when actually I'm feeling insecure about disturbing anyone. I have been hurt by reaching out, but I need to try to feel your essence, and I need to try to stop being scared to reach you.

Some Do's and Don'ts from my own personal experience

Don't assume (As already discussed)

Don't throw BPD around in an argument

PLEASE DO NOT USE MY illness against me. We have been open and honest with you about what we deal with. Yes, it may be the illness to "blame," but please don't blame everything on the illness, or on me, in a blanket careless fashion. If we are having an argument, and you want to use this as a point in the discussion, let it be a point made respectfully.

Don't expect an unrealistic sense of equality. Equality is not about sameness

I AM SENSITIVE AND intense – but you may not naturally be that way – so do not match my level of intensity or sensitivity because we will not be able to cope in this way. Be who and how you are. I know this is not an easy task, and that you may be provoked into higher levels of emotion, but I am pointing out that it is helpful for us to be who we are, and to try not to mirror each other especially when the qualities may not be helpful.

Equality and fairness is to accept each of us for who we are. I need a sense of understanding with regard to my personality, like you may need a sense of understanding with regard to something else. I agree to give and take, but it should not be unrealistic in the sense of assuming we have the same needs. We have different needs. For example, you may need space while I may need reassurance – we may need to work on how to satisfy both those needs.

Please don't fire back when I'm triggered

WHEN YOU RECOGNIZE that I'm triggered, please try not to fire back. Hurt requires compassion. If the hurt is met with more hurt then we may create a war zone. If you think, "Here we go again," wave me down, or roll your eyes at me, I will likely read these reactions as you not recognizing that what I deal with is real. This exacerbates a bad situation. If you keep reacting to my triggers, we may never stop fighting, and the intensity could damage our relationship.

I recognize that you will be triggered at times, because being human, we all have our issues that trigger us. I think it is less harmful for one of us to be triggered at a time, if at all possible. This means the non-triggered person (whether this is the person with a mental illness or not) has to attempt to hold space with understanding and compassion for the other. And if we do fire back and forth, I personally do not find it helpful (I find it more triggering!) to retrace the steps, and to figure it all out. Triggers are generally about our core issues and often not about what we are fighting over. So, who said what can be a superficial approach. If we do not deal with core issues lovingly, they are likely just going to keep coming up. We have already spoken about resolving issues, and I am not suggesting that issues are left unresolved.

Don't commit to me if you do not see me as worth the effort in the hard times. There will inevitably be hard times

IF YOU ARE GETTING into a romantic relationship with me, you need to understand that I have some complicated issues. It is not likely going to work out for us if you do not see me as worth the effort in the inevitable hard times. And I do mean the hard times brought about by BPD. I know that there are hard times for everyone else too. But I want you to recognize that this has its own set of challenges, and I do not want to feel an added sense of guilt for needing support.

I would rather not be in a partnership than be in one with someone who wants to pretend I do not need support. I can't run away from a partner every time I am not okay because that is unexpected and often! Besides, I already run away from others, and I'd like a safe space where I can just be. Will you be able to stay? You may need space of course, but do you want to try to handle things together? If you're not sure, you do not have to get involved with me. You can get involved in a situation that is calmer. It will have a set of problems of its own, but it's likely to be less emotionally intense than those you will have with me.

Don't ignore me if I'm suicidal

THIS HAS ALREADY COME up in our conversation, but it is important for it to be included under a "don't". If I mention suicide in general discussion, I may be depressed and exploring this unhealthy thinking pattern. Do not downplay suicidal ideation in people with BPD (or with anyone). Seek professional support.

Don't use BPD clichés on me

UNDERSTANDING THE ILLNESS is important, but using clichés to make sense of me is not helpful, because clichés, although they can have truth, are not relevant to every single situation. Clichéd assumption makes me lose trust in people as I realize they are looking at me like a book they read, and not at ME. Hello, here I am! I noticed that after people read a little about BPD they accused me of being manipulative, yet they never thought that before. Do they find me to be manipulative as a person, or is that someone else's framework of making sense of the diagnosis? Just because people have created a container to box a set of situations into, that does not guarantee that they understand the contents of that container correctly. And each of us is different. Manipulation sounds like a character judgment that cannot be made unless you know a person.

Do be honest with me

I DO NOT WANT INSINCERITY any more than anyone else wants that in relationships. Yes, rejection hurts, but lies hurt more in the long run. I do choose reality although it can be tough to handle.

Do respect me

RESPECT ME AS A REAL person, not just a person with a BPD lens or mental illness mask, but as a complex unique individual.

Do respect yourself

I CANNOT ALWAYS KNOW what you need and want in a relationship, and if something is too much or too little for you, you do need to assert that honestly. If you think I need someone to lovingly sit with me and have a coffee chat every morning in bed, that's great – but here is the catch – that is only great for us if YOU want that too. It is sustainable only if it is sincere, and only if you consider us both.

Do expect apologies and do give apologies

IMPULSIVITY LEADS TO rash actions and words. I do not think it is okay. It does happen with close others, and it does lead to heartfelt apologies. It isn't easy knowing you've said something you shouldn't have said, or didn't mean, to someone you care for. It is very hard accepting that you have hurt someone you love.

Apologies will come because of the impulsivity. Impulsivity means that there is a difficulty in pausing between the impulse and the (re)action. Imagine if you were to act on every impulse? Can you see how you would be apologizing and regretting things? When you do something wrong, it is likely not impulsive. But will you be apologizing too? I am expecting that most people in my life will apologize to me a lot less than I will (if they ever will). Writing that makes me feel like a bad person. Sigh.

Anyway, when you have done something that has hurt me, an apology will go a long way. I have an ability to hear and accept apologies because I know what it's like to be imperfect. It becomes difficult and imbalanced when everything is blamed on one person. This deepens an existing wound and reinforces worthless feelings. It does take two to tango particularly in partnership type relationships, where the dance is between two people who often have their two respective shadows close by. So... dinner for four, please James!

In family situations, there is sometimes a toxic or somewhat unhealthy environment that contributed towards the illness in the first place. That environment likely affected the rest of the family too as they are part of an imperfect system. I am not saying everyone else is mentally ill too, but I am saying that we have to recognize how we all interact with each other, and that we should try not to blame everything on one person. I am often taking all the blame myself, and sometimes I am willing to walk away and remove myself from family circles, thinking I am all bad. But all bad and all good do not exist – the field is gray.

Don't walk on eggshells rather learn to understand instead of watching your words

"Instead of trying to find the correct answer, try to discover and develop the correct understanding of each other".
I KNOW YOU MAY FEEL like you are walking on eggshells. It isn't helpful when people watch their words or use practiced phrases they've learned. My intuition picks up when someone is insincere. Often I get this, "ok," "ok," "ok," response when I am

upset, and I know nothing is "ok," so I don't understand why "ok" is the response. I think it may have to do with someone being afraid to say the wrong thing. But saying the wrong or right thing is not that important. I am not looking for lies.

I am looking for something real, with kindness yes, but not lies. I am mostly looking to connect with a real person. If someone gives me a fake response just to appease me, it can often have the opposite effect. I feel that people are too busy to delve into real conversations much of the time – too busy wanting good experiences to deepen the discussion to the point of resolution. But rehearsed responses are not received well by me. Yes, I know, another catch 22 because if you know I will get triggered by the truth, well then what do you do? I am sorry that I do not know. But the lie is going to trigger me TOO. Wouldn't you rather have had the chance to speak your truth?

Try to come to an understanding with each other in the relationship. Instead of trying to find the correct answer, try to discover and develop the correct understanding of each other. Then the words will hopefully not get in the way. Maybe it can be resolved with a hug. An inside out approach, maybe. Quick fixes from books, even this one, will not be enough with complex people like me and you.

Chapter 4: I want you to take care of yourself

I tried to talk about US throughout, so I hope you don't feel that your section is too small. This book was written entirely for you, and not for those with BPD. But in this section, let's address the subject of YOU very directly, and particularly of you taking care of you.

This is the best thing anyone can do for those they love – take care of yourself and your own emotional state.

I know that sometimes one with BPD tends to be perceived as a damsel in distress, no matter any outward independence. There is often an undertone of damsel lurking beneath. Do not be tempted to put your needs aside. Do not focus solely on the damsel with BPD. This is not sustainable, and not healthy for you (or him or her).

Be willing to accept your own limits, and to be honest about these. I do not expect any one person to be able to fulfill all my needs all the time. I do wish it was possible, but I know it is unfair. I do not want to be a burden. If someone pretends to be Superman, I may not see the pretense until the façade falls apart. I do not know if I will ever fall into this pattern again, given that I now distrust that anyone truly wants to be a knight. Some things are too good to be true. A knight in shining armor is not reality. A partner in crime is better ☺ . Just kidding.

But I am not kidding about the importance of balance. I do not want to be okay at your expense. If it's not obvious, I am stating it – I care about you, and I want you to be okay. I think space should be part of the self-care kit for anyone wanting to partner with me. I said it before, but I am reiterating here because it is important FOR YOU. I am trying to learn about boundaries but it is not something that comes easily to me, so if you can set your boundaries and respect them that would be good for you. Do this from a place of love for yourself. I hope you will be pleasantly surprised at how I will respect you for it.

Relationships that include you, have to consider you. If you feel unseen, talk to me about it, and address it as your need and your concern. It is not all about me in my eyes, and it should not be all about me in your eyes either – I know I am full of problems – but I do see that we are both human beings going through each of our different challenges on our journeys. You are important to me, and you should be important to yourself.

If BPD in our lives is something you do not feel you can handle by yourself, or just with me, then reach out for support. It is a complex situation, and it's more than understandable if you need support in the form of therapy, counseling, etc. to support you in dealing with someone with BPD. Being with someone so emotional may bring out your own triggers more, and therapy may be very helpful in coming to terms with your own emotions. Emotional people can unwittingly bring out the worst, but also the best, in others.

Finally, at risk of chasing you away, let me honestly say that you are absolutely a free man or woman – if BPD is just too much for you, then do not get too involved. Walk away. Yes, I will be hurt. Hurt is part of life. You are under no special obligation to stay with someone because they are dealing with BPD or dealing with anything else. Your life is yours, and you decide who you surround yourself with. Whether you are a friend, family, potential spouse, or partner, you can still decide who to keep in your life, and who to walk away from.

Besides, I am an emotional person who wants real love in my life. I want to be with someone who really likes being with me too ☺ I do not doubt that my people are out there, so if you ain't one of 'em don't worry. It will all fall into place. You do what you need to do.

Chapter 5: Stigma

I once had an experience in an ER after I impulsively took an overdose. I was in my early twenties, and I didn't understand why I did what I did. It was before my diagnosis. I remember feeling confused, overwhelmed, and very ill. It was in the days when the process was volatile to get things out of your system, and I was struggling to say the least. I was crying too. A nurse was there telling me I was wasting her time as she could have been saving someone who wanted to live instead. I didn't know it was possible to feel worse, but I felt worse when I heard that.

I seem to have blocked out a lot of these traumatic experiences that make me feel shame. But that one I remember clearly, and it depicts the state of the "help" that is offered to someone with severe mental illness. It depicts the stigma that makes people hide their mental illness. This stigma prevents support, prevents sharing of real stories of success and growth, prevents people from reaching out for help, stifles awareness, and ultimately leads to more fatalities. When I hear of a teenager committing suicide, I want to be brave enough to stand up in a school and talk about the reality of mental illness and suicidal ideation. I want to remove the shame and be part of the solution. But my experiences make me afraid. Will I be emotionally stoned?

Many of the stories I write here are stories that those close to me have not heard. My family knows things went horribly wrong, but they do not know the extent of my pain and experiences. They do not know that although I seem okay I am still fighting a daily battle. They do not know what I mean when

I say that I'm busy and can't make dinner, or lunch, or a concert. They think I am strong, or they think I am weak, they think I am in control either way. I cannot easily call on my family for their support because I fear being shamed, misunderstood, or rejected. Besides, I want to be the one to be there for them, and I do not want to worry them. I want to be able to take care of myself, and I am still trying and failing.

I am afraid that if they believed some of the hate speech online about my illness then they may change their minds about loving me. Sometimes I feel like I am living a lie by not telling them plainly what I deal with, and sometimes I feel like I would not want to die without being fully open with those closest to me. Some may know, but we do not speak openly about it. Then I consider that my family didn't choose me. I have been honest and open with my partners when I entered into relationships, so that they could have the choice as to whether to get involved with me or not. I don't tell many of my friends, but I keep them at arm's length, so I don't feel like they need to know.

I sometimes feel that I may somehow be giving myself permission to *be* a person with Borderline in all my relationships if everyone in my life knew about it. Maybe this lack of conversation about it protects my relationships. This diagnosis has a strange feeling – in ways, it has helped me and given me hope from the answers it brought. In other ways, it makes me hopeless because of all the stigma surrounding it, and because of the intense view people have of BPD.

It almost sounds like someone with BPD came up with the diagnosis – it's black and white, and intense. I even wonder if we manifest more drama from the very diagnosis. This diagnosis is definitely one that one wants to start growing out of as soon as one comes to terms with it! And luckily, I am blessed with a few gems online who have managed to convince me that there definitely is hope, that many people with Borderline lead healthy lives, and even that we have our strengths like artistic talents that come from the intensity of emotion. There are celebrities who live with BPD. These people are admired by the world. Is it their hurt that moved them to such heights of expression? Perspective makes a big difference. And remember that, hey, we are not thaaaaat crazy as "they" make us out to be. After all, we are all human. We need to keep front of mind that BPD has a spectrum, and traits can be less or more severe. This is sobering to realize.

When educating yourself on BPD, it is important to find reliable resources. Research with your goal in mind – are you trying to prove the other person wrong? No. You are likely intending to improve your relationship. You will find what you are looking for. It is difficult to sift through the stigma online, but there is information and support available. The web is flooded with information. We cannot just go with every viewpoint. I believe that with guidance and good intentions on what you want to achieve from the support and information, you can find helpful information suitable for you. I have unfortunately felt disappointed by many experts online (and offline). I appreciate that other experts have set things straight with tremendous insight, support, perspective, tools, and good energy.

Imagined and Unimagined hurt. Please stay with me

I EXPLAINED HOW I IMAGINED the abandonment from an ex-boyfriend. I also realized while writing this to you, how I had imagined an overall pattern of my partners abandoning me when in fact it was me who ended most of my relationships. This makes me feel – sick. It is understandable to me now that people take this understanding and apply it more generally to their understanding of BPD thereby assuming that we imagine everything. I want to say two things here. The first is that imagined hurt still hurts as the mind and body do not quite know the difference. The second is that there is an unimagined part or parts. I also want to draw attention here to the spectrum of BPD and remind us that this mental illness occurs on a spectrum. Symptoms and traits may be strongly triggered, dormant, or somewhere in between. We need to consider that reality is often in between with episodes of extremes.

I want to mention briefly the initial abandonment which was real. Initially in my life, my mother was my favorite person in the whole world, possibly like mothers are to most children. I was already intensely emotional before she left. People say I clung to her, and that I would not let others close to me, or to her. I was closely attached to her. I wonder whether I intuitively knew that she was going to leave, and if I was trying to hold onto her to make her stay. That may sound far-fetched, but my feelings say it could be. She left and took my memory of her away too. I do not remember what it was like. Those years of closeness to her are gone. This abandonment and subsequent childhood abuse and neglect were not imagined.

I do see situations in my adult life where I have imagined pending abandonment. There have been times where I was too afraid that someone would leave because things felt too good to be true – a false belief that it could not be real that someone would love me and commit to loving me for... forever. I only see this reality in hindsight, years later.

I have seen inside my heart. I walked into my open heart as it has been broken open. I found sharp tainted pieces. I put them together like a puzzle that my life depends on. They became a mosaic mirror. And I looked at myself. I reflected, and I reflected. Until I saw deep experiences of love, lessons, and life. I am shattered by what I see, but grateful for the lessons that have helped me grow and discover I am worthy of love, and so are you.

I see now, that in my love life, I have experienced the bliss of love, only to run from it out of fear of being let down. This I see as imagined abandonment; perceived but not real rejection.

I see how I recreated the later years of my childhood of emotional abuse and neglect by attracting abusive or emotionally unavailable partners.

Together we replayed the movie of my life with stunning accuracy (and perhaps theirs too, from their perspective). These are not imagined hurts. The abuse and neglect in relationships has been real. I see that it resulted in part from my unconscious attractions out of my story, my fears, and my false beliefs.

In hindsight, when I am clear-minded and brave, I look with intense honesty, and I see it in all its vivid reality. I can hardly believe the way it all fits together.

I ask myself what comes next. I ask myself, now that I seem to have played it all out and found myself an adult with nothing left to relive, can we start creating a new and better story? I hope so. It has been an exhausting journey. I am tired. Maybe my next relationship will last, but should there be no next relationship, I am eternally grateful for the pieces of my heart that everyone on my journey has contributed to helping me find.

I am only human

BPD CAN BE A SEVERE illness when it is on the severe end of the spectrum. I have been on the severe end of the spectrum. I am still experiencing strong traits of the disorder, but I feel a lot less in its grips than I have been in earlier years. I'm able to make attempts at changes. I have hope. In the face of this hope, I have to say that we cannot be the only ones with problems and deep despair. We are all human, and the world is full of despair. BPD creates intense emotional states. Yet every person is emotional and has the capacity for these emotional states, both high and low. We are not that different. We are not monsters. But sometimes we behave like children. Sometimes I love being like a child, but I know I have to be both the child and the parent to myself. We are just grown-up girls and boys like you. We are all trying. We all have problems, and every relationship involves more than just one person. There are many people on the planet, and you can choose who your people are that make you feel what you want to feel ☺ I want to feel it all. I want to embrace life for what it is. I want to embrace myself for who I am. As Pink so aptly says in her 'Just like Fire' song, "No one can be just like me anyway!"

Misconceptions

I AM HOPING THAT BY now in our conversation, we agree that BPD is hardly the fatal attraction scenario portrayed by the media. Perhaps it is possible that someone could develop such severe reactions, given zero awareness, zero support, or no desire to heal. However, labels, boxes, and stories of one person instead of the story of your person are only helpful up to a point, and then become unhelpful. I think it is better to take what you can, can what you can't, and go and get to know your loved one and yourself more, so that you can together create a safe space and some improvements to your relationship if you want your relationship to thrive. Many have made it work, and they talk about it like any other relationship with love and understanding.

The manipulation misconception

WHEN I EXAMINE A DISCUSSION in hindsight, with much effort, I can be open to how someone may think I am manipulative. This kind of discussion has happened to me in romantic relationships. I can understand how someone may have thought that I was pretending to be intensely upset while asking them to please stay. I do not pretend to be intense. I am intense. I do not pretend to be afraid of abandonment. Sometimes I am intensely afraid. The misconception here is that I am acting, so that I can get something from you. There is no act at that stage (pardon the pun), not that I act at any other stage either. I do not expect any specific thing from you after I express my fears or my pain to you. Ironically, BPD type beliefs expect nothing from you in those heightened moments of being triggered.

I get that my reactions can be intense, and can seem inappropriate to a situation. They can be "unreasonable" by the general standard of emotional reactions. I am asking if you can get that I am not trying to be, nor wanting to be unreasonable, and I am not trying to hurt anyone. I am dealing with a valid problem with my brain! If we can get that judgment out of the way, my brain may find it easier to relax and allow me to control it.

The incurable misconception

THERE ARE VIEWS THAT BPD is incurable. Some information you may read may suggest that the illness is lifelong. But some experts will say that their patients improve with time, effort, therapy, hope, and support. I favor the hopeful. In my personal journey, my experience has been one of change. I had problems when I was 20, and I have problems at 40, but there have been changes, insights, growth, and improvements in my life. Some of these changes involved trying to craft a lifestyle that works for me – one that involves more space to myself and more flexibility, so that I can try to care for my needs more effectively. I have moments where I make peace with it all, thinking that I am going through lessons my soul wants to learn. My spiritual perspective of the journey helps me to embrace life despite the seeming chaos or emotional instability. To me, perspective is miraculous. And, there are definitely ups also, not just downs.

Chapter 6: Conclusion

I hope this helps you to find some clarity, strength, and perspective. Thank you for investing your time to learn about what your significant other, family member, or friend is going through. Thank you for being part of the journey, and for opening up to different perspectives about BPD. I know that some people like me, may not be able to speak so openly to those close to them, yet we could write it for strangers more easily. And I am really grateful that you've read this.

I hope you get to know each other better and better, and with mutual growing respect, acceptance, love, openness, support, and connection. I would like to leave you with some inspiration by giving you a glimpse of the intense emotions on the other side... the good emotions... the highs I experience as part of life. My moods swing, my experiences swing, my experiences can be heart-breaking suffering, but they can also be beautiful joy beyond anything I could capture in words. Sometimes I am alone, sometimes I am with another, sometimes I am dreaming asleep, or walking, or talking, and all of a sudden, the beauty arrives.

The remarkably intensely beautiful emotions are the other side of the coin. Suffice to say that I've often felt like the happiest person alive from listening to a tune, admiring a piece of emotional art that speaks to my soul, watching a bird, playing in the rain, having a perfect moment of laughter with someone I love, falling in love, getting a heartfelt hug, giving a smile to a child, watching someone I love grow, watching someone I love be happy, having a dream of a beautiful animal I love, feeling the sea when I look at it, feeling like I am the waterfall when I watch it, and everything that goes with being on the inside of a mind and heart that feel every drop of life around it – the good, the bad, and the ugly, but oh the beautiful too! I experience heights of joy that make me truly blessed. My personality and my life have a beautiful side to it too. It is every color, and sometimes I do love that... how could I not! It may be how I somehow get through the hard times.

Take care of yourself. And be alive in your own true colors.

Don't miss out!

Visit the website below and you can sign up to receive emails whenever K. Marie publishes a new book. There's no charge and no obligation.

https://books2read.com/r/B-A-DEDX-QLANC

BOOKS 2 READ

Connecting independent readers to independent writers.

Also by K. Marie

Carta de una Mujer con Trastorno Límite de la Personalidad
Letter from a Woman with Borderline Personality Disorder

Watch for more at https://www.caoshermoso.com.

About the Author

K. Marie, born and raised in the beautiful island of Puerto Rico, where she still resides with her husband, was diagnosed with Bipolar Disorder Type 2, ADHD and BPD Traits in 2018. She is an advocate for mental health and strives to share her experience with others. You can form part of her community on Instagram and Facebook: @caoshermoso, where you can ask questions, learn more and share your own experiences.

Read more at https://www.caoshermoso.com.